About the Author

Mr. Paul Watson has many years of experience in working with Selenium and Appium. He has worked on large software projects in USA, UK, Singapore, Hong Kong, Dubai, Australia and Switzerland.

His hobbies include travelling to new tourist places, watching basketball, cricket, Soccer and learning latest technological stuff.

Who is this book for

This book is for software developers, automation testers, Devops and engineers working on IT project. Whether you are a beginner or an experienced developer, this book will help you master the skills on Appium.

The book starts with introduction of Appium and then dives into key concepts like creating appium project in IntelliJ IDEA, automating the native, hybrid and web Android as well as iOS applications. The book also covers advanced gestures like swiping, zooming, pinching, tapping operations as well. Book also covers how you can run your test on virtual devices as well as real phones.

Preface

In this book, you will learn below topics.

1. Introduction
2. Appium protocol
3. Android Concepts
4. Android Environment set up
5. Capabilities for Android Automation
6. Inspecting elements
7. Android Web apps
8. Testing older Android apps using Selendroid in Appium
9. Adding dependency for AndroidDriver
10. Testing a native android application
11. Automating basic tasks
12. Testing the hybrid Android application
13. Important classes in Appium library
14. Complex actions in Appium
15. Android Emulator Automation
16. Registering appium (Android node) with Selenium grid
17. Setting up Appium environment in Mac OS X
18. Appium app on Mac OS, Appium doctor
19. Simulators in XCode
20. Capabilities for iOS automation
21. Inpsecting the elements from Appium inspector
22. Automating Native iOS app
23. Automating Hybrid app
24. Automating Web app,
25. Hooking up appium with Selenium grid

Android Automation Testing

1. Introduction

Market share of Android devices is growing day by day and so the need for quality applications.

All major organisations around the world are launching the Android applications to gain the upper hand in business. Similarly, the dynamics of web applications is also changing. Technology officers want their websites to be rendered properly on all kinds of platforms be it desktop, tablets, mobile phones, iPads or iPhones.

Manually testing Android applications is a tedious and boring process. So companies are moving towards automation tools like Appium. Earlier Selendroid was used for automation of Android devices with API level < 17. Below screenshot shows the API levels of Android.

Platform Version	API Level	VERSION_CODE	Notes
Android 6.0	23	M	API Changes
Android 5.1	22	LOLLIPOP_MR1	Platform Highlights
Android 5.0	21	LOLLIPOP	
Android 4.4W	20	KITKAT_WATCH	KitKat for Wearables Only
Android 4.4	19	KITKAT	Platform Highlights
Android 4.3	18	JELLY_BEAN_MR2	Platform Highlights
Android 4.2, 4.2.2	17	JELLY_BEAN_MR1	Platform Highlights
Android 4.1, 4.1.1	16	JELLY_BEAN	Platform Highlights
Android 4.0.3, 4.0.4	15	ICE_CREAM_SANDWICH_MR1	Platform Highlights
Android 4.0, 4.0.1, 4.0.2	14	ICE_CREAM_SANDWICH	
Android 3.2	13	HONEYCOMB_MR2	
Android 3.1.x	12	HONEYCOMB_MR1	Platform Highlights
Android 3.0.x	11	HONEYCOMB	Platform Highlights

2. Appium protocol

Appium uses native automation frameworks of Apple and Android.

1. UIAutomation by Apple
2. UiAutomator or Instrumentation by Android

On the top, Appium uses Selenium WebDriver API which uses JSON Wire Protocol. So we can write our tests in any language like C#, Java, Python, PHP, Ruby as we webdriver client
API are available in these languages. You can get these libraries from http://appium.io/downloads

Appium receives commands from selenium client and then forwards these commands to Android or Apple Automator. Android or Apple automator executes these commands and sends response back to the Appium server.

Below command shows the Appium architecture.

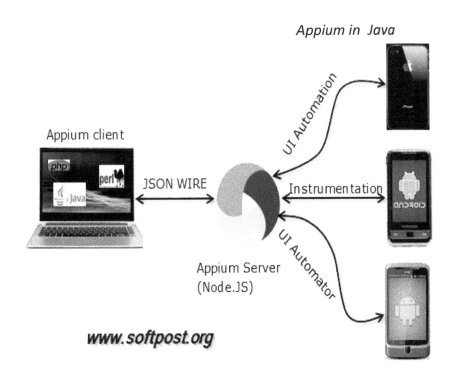

Appium architecture

3. Android Concepts

3.1 Types of android applications

There are 3 types of Android applications.

1. Native Applications
2. Web Applications
3. Hybrid Applications

Examples -

Native applications are those that are installed from the .apk files. The calculator that you use on Android is a native application.

Web application is any website that you can view on browser in Android. So all websites that you can access on your mobile phone are web applications from Android perspective.

Hybrid applications are combinations of native applications and web applications. For example - Subway Surfer game is a hybrid application because it allows you to switch to browser mode and access facebook and come back.

3.2 Basics of Android OS

Before we dive in to the interesting world of Android automation, let us try to understand some basics of the Android mobile phone.

You need to know below things on your Android phone.

1. Android version
2. Device Name
3. Developer Options
4. Debugging mode

To find out the Android version and device name, just go to the settings of your mobile and tap on About device menu item. The About device screen will show you the version of the Android system.

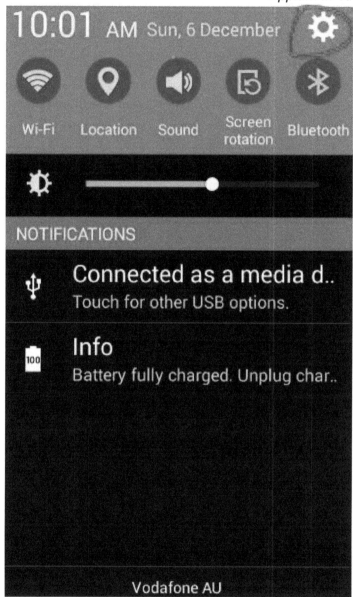

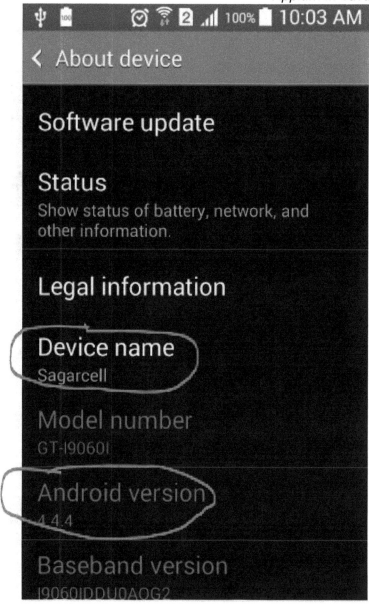

To be able to automate the Android device, you should enable the USB debugging option in Developer options screen. All new Android phones have their Developer options menu item hidden. To view the Developer options, you should tap the Build number in About device screen 7 times as shown in below image.

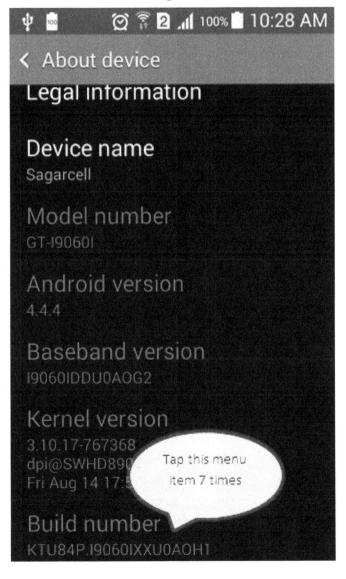

After that, you can go to settings menu and tap on the Developer options menu item.

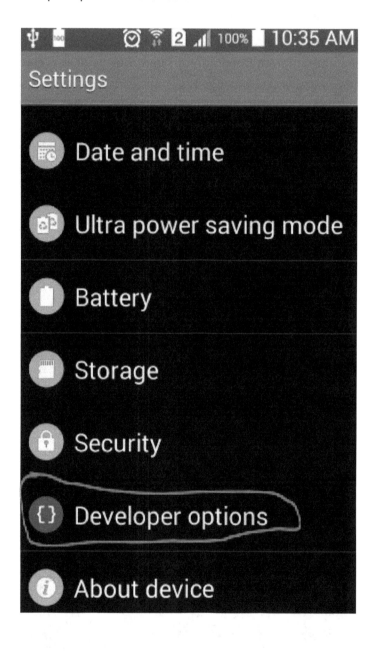

On Developer options screen, you should enable Stay awake check box on which ensures that device will not get locked while in debug mode. Also ensure that you check USB debugging option on which allows Appium to interact with mobile.

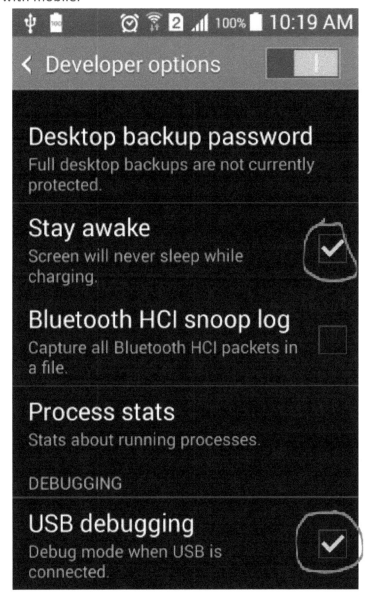

4. Android Environment set up

4.1 Installation of Android SDK

You need to download and install below tools.

1. JDK
2. Android SDK tools

Android SDK is the tool kit developed by Google for developing the applications for Android OS.
SDK tools include below tools.

1. AVD Manager – used for managing the virtual devices (Emulators)
2. Debugger - DDMS, ADB
3. Android Libraries

Once you download the Android SDK, go to the installation directory and open SDK Manager.

SDK Manager allows you to download and install the Android tools like ADB, emulator, API libraries, Monitor, DDMS etc.

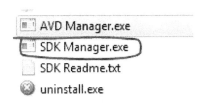

Android SDK Manager - Settings

Proxy Settings

HTTP Proxy Server

HTTP Proxy Port |

Manifest Cache

Directory:

Current Size: 549 KiB

☑ Use download cache

Clear Cache

Others

☐ Force https://... sources to be fetched using http://...

☐ Ask before restarting ADB

☑ Enable Preview Tools

Below image shows Android SDK manager window.

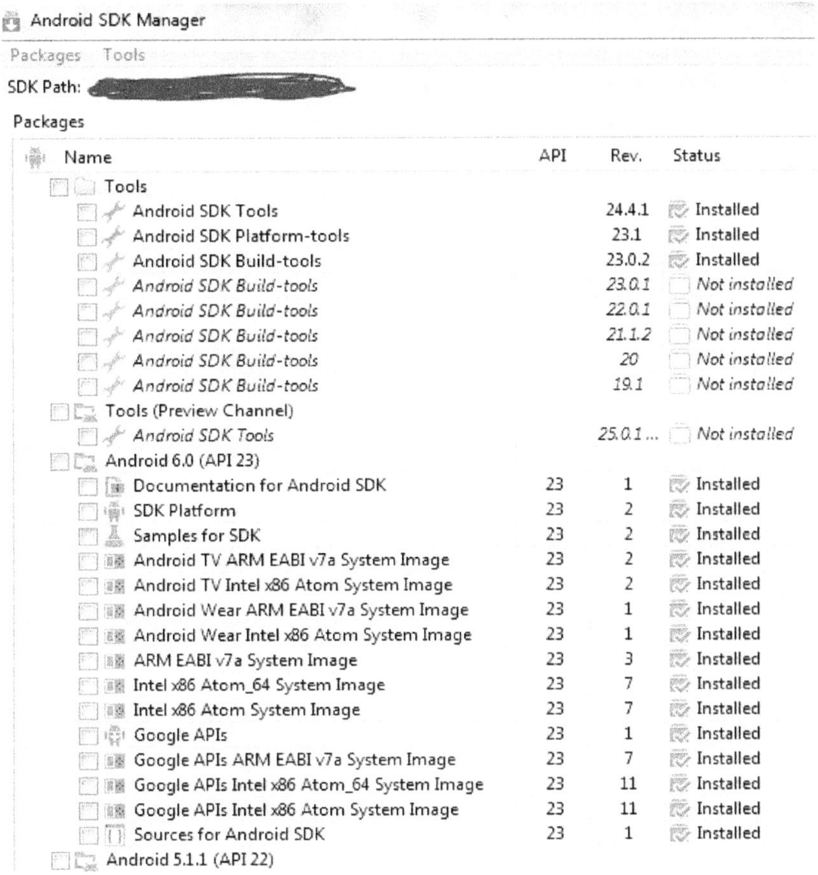

SDK manager allows you to install/uninstall build tools and Android API libraries. You can see which tools are installed in Status column. To install specific tool, just select the checkbox in front of the tool and click on install. The requested packages will be downloaded and installed in your installation directory. If you are behind the proxy, you will have to provide the proxy server details in below screen. You can access proxy details window by clicking on Tools->options menu in above window.

After installation of all SDK tools, my Android SDK directory looks like below.

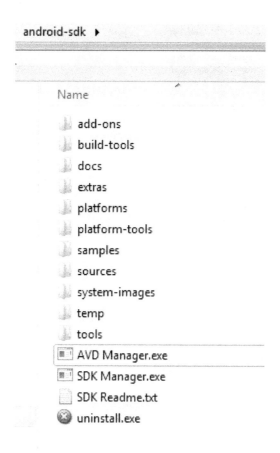

Tools folder looks like below. It contains many important tools like DDMS, emulator, monitor, monkey runner, android etc.

android-sdk ▶ tools ▶

Name

📁 ant
📁 apps
📁 bin
📁 lib
📁 proguard
📁 qemu
📁 support
📁 templates
⚙️ android.bat
⚙️ ddms.bat
⚙️ draw9patch.bat
🪦 emulator.exe
🪦 emulator64-ranchu-arm64.exe
🪦 emulator64-ranchu-mips64.exe
🪦 emulator-arm.exe
🪦 emulator-mips.exe
🪦 emulator-ranchu-arm64.exe
🪦 emulator-ranchu-mips64.exe
🪦 emulator-x86.exe
⚙️ hierarchyviewer.bat
⚙️ jobb.bat
⚙️ lint.bat
▪️ mksdcard.exe
⚙️ monitor.bat
⚙️ monkeyrunner.bat
📄 NOTICE.txt
📄 source.properties
⚙️ traceview.bat
⚙️ uiautomatorviewer.bat

24

Platform-tools folder contains important debug tool called as ADB.

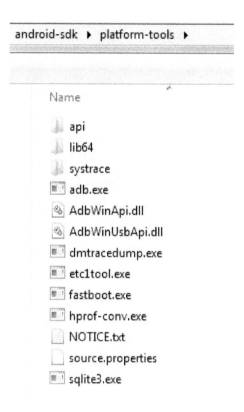

4.2 Installation and configuration of Appium and Android tools

In this topic, let us take a look at what tools you will need to install to be able to work with Android automation.

Below is the list of tools you will need for automation.

1. Appium server
2. Android SDK
3. Java JDK and JRE
4. Maven
5. Java IDE (Eclipse or Intellij IDEA)
6. Android Mobile phone (I am using Samsung Duos)

Once you install above tools, ensure that update path variable on your windows system to include all tools as mentioned below.

1. JDK tools
2. Maven tools
3. Android SDK tools and platform tools

Sample path might look like "G:\apache-maven-3.2.3\bin;F:\selenium;D:\android\bin;D:\android\sdk\platform-tools;D:\android\sdk\tools"

You also need to create new environment variables as mentioned below.

1. JAVA_HOME (e.g. C:\Program
   Files\Java\jdk1.8.0_11)
2. JRE_HOME (e.g. C:\Program Files\Java\jre1.8.0_40)
3. ANDROID_HOME (e.g. D:\android\sdk)
4. M2_MAVEN (e.g. G:\apache-maven-3.2.3)

4.3 Registering your mobile phone with Android device manager

Before installing Appium, I recommend you register your Android device with your laptop or desktop using below steps.

1. Enable the USB debugging on your mobile phone in developer options.
2. Attach your mobile phone to your laptop or desktop using USB cable.
3. Once you attach mobile, drivers will be installed on your system and **RSA KEY** will be added into your mobile phone. Just accept the key on your mobile. This completes the registration process.
4. You can check if mobile is registered or not by going to **Android monitor** or by running command **adb devices** from command prompt.

Sometimes, we face driver issues while registering the mobile with Android device manager. For example, when I was trying to register my Samsung Duos with system, adb devices command returned empty results. To fix this

problem, I installed the device driver for mobile by
following below steps which fixed my problem.

1. Go to the device manager of your system.
2. Right click on your device and click on update
   device driver.
3. Select browse my computer.
4. Select let me pick from the list of device drivers.
5. Install Samsung Android ADB Interface as shown in
   below screen

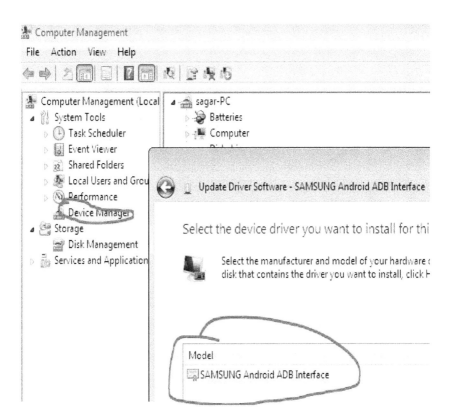

After that you can see your device in your Android device
manager.

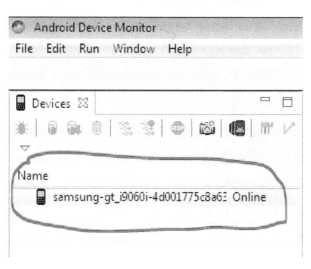

4.4 Understanding the Android SDK tools like adb, Monitor, UIAutomator

Now that you have registered your mobile phone with your system, it's the time to play around with it using Android SDK tools.

The ultimate tool to know is Android device monitor. It is located in tools directory in your Android SDK. (e.g. D:\android\sdk\tools\Monitor.bat). Just double click on it and it will launch the Android Device Monitor as shown in below image.

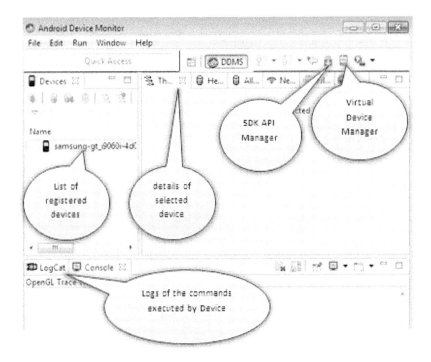

Device monitor also allows you to take the screenshots from your mobile or view the applications internal element structure.

Below image shows how you can take screenshot of the mobile screen in device monitor.

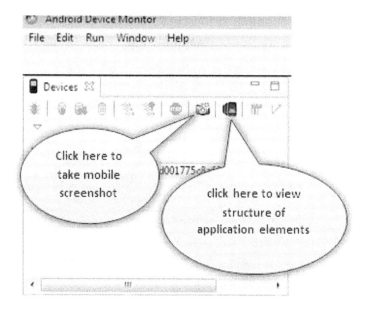

4.5 Popular adb commands

Here is the list of popular adb commands that can be used to send commands to apps on Android device.

Starting the app on Android device

adb shell am start -n com.android.calculator2/.Calculator

Listing all packages in the device

adb shell pm list packages

Listing only system packages in the device

adb shell pm list packages -s

Viewing the activity intents in the device

adb shell dumpsys activity intents

Viewing the activity broadcasts in the device

adb shell dumpsys activity broadcasts

Here is the list of more ADB commands.

1. **adb devices** : Command to view Android devices attached to computer
2. **adb install xyz.apk** : ommand to install Android app on Android Emulator
3. **adb pull /sdcard/abc.png** : command to pull files from Android emulator to machine
4. **adb shell input text 'any text'** : command to enter value in text
5. **adb shell am start -a android.intent.action.VIEW** : ADB Shell command to start the activity in Android Emulator
6. **adb shell pm list packages** : How to print all packages within Emulator?
7. **adb shell pm uninstall com.example.MyApp** : command to uninstall app in Android Emulator
8. **adb shell screencap /sdcard/screen.png** : Taking the screenshot

9. **adb shell screenrecord /sdcard/demo.mp4 :** to record an Android Emulator screen. Recording can be stopped by pressing ctrl+c or we can also set the time limit

10. **adb shell ls /system/bin :** To display all commands

11. **adb shell start avd1 :** Command to start the device

5. Appium Server

5.1 Working with Appium Server

Once you have got your mobile registered with Android device manager, you can launch Appium server.

Below screenshot shows how Appium server GUI looks like.

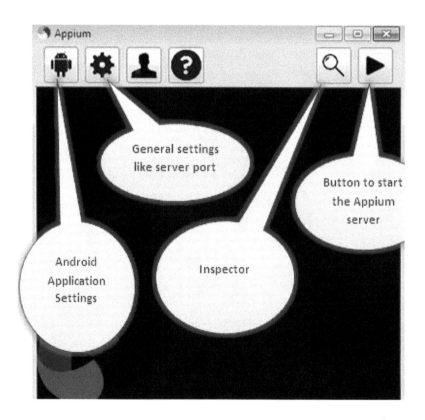

Hit the start button and server will start running right away. Below screen shot shows the log after the server is up and running.

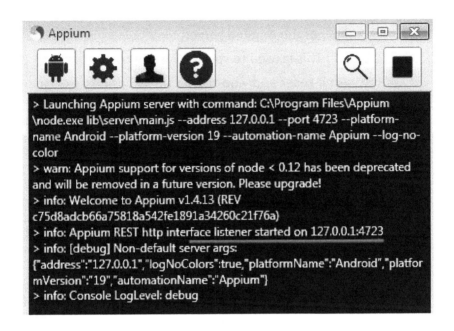

5.2 Appium server arguments

We can start the Appium server using below arguments

1. **-a and -p :** This is used to specify the address and port of the Appium server
2. **-U :** This is used to specify the device id
3. **--full-reset and --no-reset :** These options are used to specify if we want to reinstall the app before starting testing. When we choose full-reset option, app is reinstalled.
4. **--app :** This is used to specify the application path
5. **--session-override :** This is used to specify if want to override the sessions. Usually only one session is allowed. If other session is created, we get error saying SessionNotCreatedException: A new session could not be created. (Original error: Requested a new session but one was in progress) To avoid such errors, we can use this argument with value as true.
6. **--app-pkg and --app-activity :** This is used to specify the package and activity of the Android app to be launched
7. **--platform-name and --platform-version :** These options are used to specify the platform name and version to be used for automation
8. **--device-name :** This is used to specify the name of device
9. **--automation-name :** This is used to specify if we want to use Appium or Selendroid

10. **--browser-name :** This is used to specify the browser to be used for the automation

11. **--nodeconfig :** This is used to pass the node configuration to used with selenium grid

12. **--orientation :** Device orientation to be used

6. Capabilities for Android Automation

6.1 Capabilities for Android application

We can pass below capabilities to automate the Android app.

1. platformName
2. platformVersion
3. deviceName
4. app
5. browserName
6. newCommandTimeout
7. autoWebview - switch to web view automatically
8. appActivity
9. appPackage

6.2 How to get device name, version and app details

To automate the Android app, we should know below capability values.

1. deviceName
2. VERSION
3. appPackage
4. appActivity

You can get version and device name from About Device section in Settings of your phone.

about device in Android phone

If you have installed the app on your phone, you can use below commands to find out the package and main activity of app. Ensure that you are on home screen of your app

adb devices

adb shell

dumpsys window windows

Here is the sample screenshot of above commands.

```
  mCurConfiguration={0 1.0 505mcc3mnc en_US ldltr sw320dp w320dp h508dp 240
dpi nrml long port finger -keyb/v/h -nav/h s.16}
  mCurrentFocus=Window{42fc3350 u0 com.facebook.katana/com.facebook.katana.
LoginActivity}
  mFocusedApp=AppWindowToken{42eae388 token=Token{4319fb40 ActivityRecord{4
22f0da0 u0 com.facebook.katana/.LoginActivity t17}}}
  mInputMethodTarget=Window{43304660 u0 com.google.android.googlequicksearc
hbox/com.google.android.apps.gsa.searchnow.SearchNowActivity}
  mInTouchMode=true mLayoutSeq=16015
  mLastDisplayFreezeDuration=+461ms due to Window{435cb1b0 u0 com.google.an
droid.youtube/com.google.android.apps.youtube.app.WatchWhileActivity}
  mSystemDecorLayer=161000 mScreenRect=[0,0][480,800]
  mWallpaperTarget=null
  mLastWallpaperX=-1.0 mLastWallpaperY=-1.0
  mSystemBooted=true mDisplayEnabled=true
  mTransactionSequence=19437
  mDisplayFrozen=false windows=false client=false apps=0 waitingForConfig=f
alse
  mRotation=0 mAltOrientation=false
```

adb commands to find the app package and activity

Or you can also use APK Info app (Intelloware) to get information about other apps.

Here is the sample code snippet using above capabilities

```
capabilities.SetCapability("VERSION", "4.4.4");

capabilities.SetCapability("deviceName","yource
llname");

capabilities.SetCapability("platformName","Andr
oid");

capabilities.SetCapability("BROWSER_Name",
"Android");

capabilities.setCapability("appPackage",
"org.softpost");

capabilities.setCapability("appActivity",
"org.softpost.AbcActivity");
```

6.3 Getting the main activity of Android App

To automate the Android application, you need to specify the application package name and activity.

An Android application can have multiple activities. But we may not be able to launch all the activities. To find out the main activity, you can use below commands.

1. adb shell pm list packages -f
2. adb pull /system/app/Calculator/Calculator.apk
3. aapt dump badging Calculator.apk

First command lists all the application paths and package names. Then second command copies the apk file from the emulator or device on the machine. Finally we have used aapt tool to find the main activity of the app. **aapt tool** is inside Android SDK directory
..android-sdk\build-tools\23.0.2

Here are the screenshots of above commands.

```
Sagar@Sagar-Windows10 ~
$ adb shell pm list packages -f
package:/system/app/ringtoneBR.apk=com.sec.android.app.ringtoneBR
package:/system/priv-app/DefaultContainerService.apk=com.android.defcontainer
package:/data/app/com.tencent.mm-10.apk=com.tencent.mm
package:/system/app/SecFactoryPhoneTest.apk=com.sec.phone
package:/data/app/it.wemakeawesomesh.skitracker-1.apk=it.wemakeawesomesh.skitracker
package:/data/app/com.makemytrip-12.apk=com.makemytrip
package:/system/priv-app/FmmDS.apk=com.fmm.ds
package:/system/app/PartnerBookmarksProvider.apk=com.android.providers.partnerbookmarks
package:/system/priv-app/SecContacts_ENTRY.apk=com.android.contacts
package:/system/priv-app/SecGallery_ESS.apk=com.sec.android.gallery3d
package:/system/priv-app/TeleService_ESS.apk=com.android.phone
package:/data/app/io.appium.unlock-1.apk=io.appium.unlock
package:/system/priv-app/FotaClient.apk=com.sec.android.fotaclient
package:/system/priv-app/FmmDM.apk=com.fmm.dm
package:/system/app/SecHTMLViewer.apk=com.android.htmlviewer
package:/system/app/BluetoothTest.apk=com.sec.android.app.bluetoothtest
package:/data/app/com.kiloo.subwaysurf-13.apk=com.kiloo.subwaysurf
package:/system/app/SCParser.apk=com.sec.android.app.parser
package:/system/priv-app/GoogleLoginService.apk=com.google.android.gsf.login
package:/system/app/SamsungIME.apk=com.sec.android.inputmethod
package:/system/app/Bluetooth.apk=com.android.bluetooth
package:/system/priv-app/SecCalendarProvider_NOTSTICKER.apk=com.android.providers.calendar
package:/system/priv-app/DeviceTest.apk=com.sec.factory
package:/system/app/SPlanner_ESS.apk=com.android.calendar
package:/system/app/SecBrowser_ESS.apk=com.android.browser
package:/system/app/AntHalService.apk=com.dsi.ant.server
package:/system/app/AllshareFileShare.apk=com.sec.android.allshare.service.fileshare
package:/system/app/BadgeProvider.apk=com.sec.android.provider.badge
package:/system/app/FactoryCamera_FB.apk=com.sec.factory.camera
package:/system/app/SecDownloadProviderUi.apk=com.android.providers.downloads.ui
package:/system/app/DocumentsUI.apk=com.android.documentsui
package:/data/app/com.instagram.android-17.apk=com.instagram.android
```

list all packages from the android device

Note that above command prints the package details for all apps in the device. You can use grep command to filter only specific apps as shown in below image.

```
Sagar@Sagar-Windows10 ~
$ adb shell pm list packages -f | grep "calc"
package:/system/app/SecCalculator2_ESS.apk=com.sec.android.app.popupcalculator

Sagar@Sagar-Windows10 ~
$ adb pull /system/app/SecCalculator2_ESS.apk
3441 KB/s (297978 bytes in 0.084s)
```

Pulling the apk file of app from android device

As shown in above image, we have listed the package details for only calculator. Then we have pulled the apk file to system.

```
Sagar@Sagar-Windows10 ~
$ aapt dump badging SecCalculator2_ESS.apk | grep "launchable"
launchable-activity: name='com.sec.android.app.popupcalculator.Calculator'
```

Finding the launchable activity in Android app

Once the apk file is available, you can get the launchable activity as shown in above image.

Here are some of the main activities of apps on Android Emulator.

1. com.android.browser/.BrowserActivity
2. com.android.calculator2/.Calculator
3. com.android.dialer/.DialtactsActivity
4. com.android.contacts/.activities.PeopleActivity
5. com.google.android.apps.messaging/.ui.Conversati onListActivity
6. com.android.calendar/.AllInOneActivity
7. com.android.deskclock/.DeskClock
8. com.android.settings/.Settings
9. com.android.music/ArtistAlbumBrowserActivity

Here are the main activities of some of the popular Android apps.

1. com.flipkart.android.activity/.HomeFragmentHolde rActivity
2. com.viber.voip/.WelcomeActivity
3. com.whatsapp/.Main

Note that if you try to launch the invalid activity, you will get the error saying Permission to start activity denied.

Android app can have multiple activities. To mark the specific activity as the starting activity, you have to add the intent-filter as shown in below example. Usually developers need to add below XML section app's manifest file to make the specific activity as launchable.

```xml
<activity

android:name=".MainActivity"

android:label="XYZ">

<intent-filter>

<action
android:name="android.intent.action.MAIN" />

<category
android:name="android.intent.category.LAUNCHER"
/>

</intent-filter>

</activity>
```

7. Inspecting elements

7.1 Inspecting the elements in native Android App

We can use UI Automator in Android Monitor to inspect the elements inside app.

Below image shows that we have inspected the chat contact in WhatsApp application.

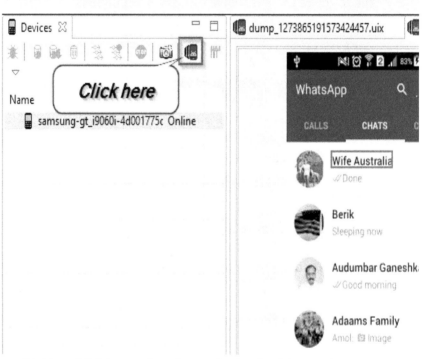

Taking UI hierarchy dump in Android monitor

Inspecting element using UI Automator in Android device monitor

From the node details, we can get properties and values of selected element. This information can be used to write XPATH expressions used to identify the elements.

48

7.2 Inspecting the elements in hybrid and web Android apps

We can use chrome to inspect the elements inside android web apps.

Ensure that you have attached the device to computer in USB mode. Also ensure that version of Android OS is 4.4 or higher. You can use **adb devices** command to check that device is connected properly.

Note that - In hybrid apps, the Webview control is used. In such cases, developer should make the debugging enabled for the Webview control. Developer needs to add below line of code at the time of initializing the Webview control.

```
if(Build.VERSION.SDK_INT >=
Build.VERSION_CODES.KITKAT)
{
WebView.setWebContentsDebuggingEnabled(true);
}
```

If the debugging is not enabled for the Webview control, chrome will not be able to inspect the elements.

Next, you have to enter below line in the chrome address bar.

chrome://inspect/#devices

Below image shows how to inspect the apps in chrome.
Note that below image shows mobile GT-I9060I is
connected to computer in debug mode. It shows the all
web and hybrid apps that are open in the Android phone.

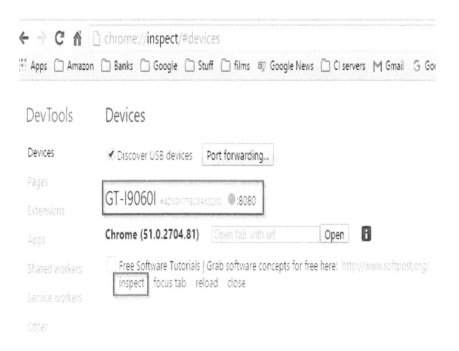

Inspecting the elements inside Android app using chrome

Once you hit inspect button, html source code is displayed as shown in below image.

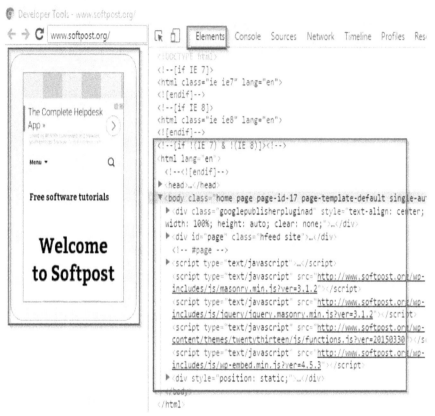

Html source of Android app in chrome

Apart from above methods, you can also use mobile emulation in chrome to inspect the elements inside web Android app as shown in below image. We can view the web app as displayed in various mobile devices like iPhone, Android Nexus, Samsung Galaxy etc.

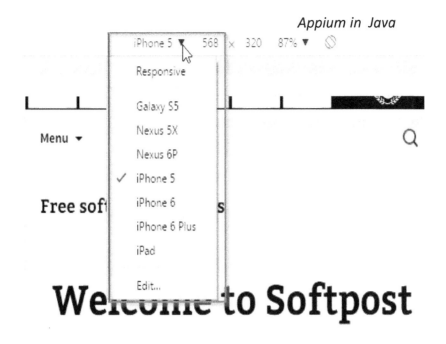

Mobile emulation in chrome

7.3 Element Identification methods

For web apps and Webview content, we can use normal selenium element identification methods.

For Native apps, we can use id, className, XPATH. But can not use link text and partial link text.

We should avoid using XPATH to identify the native controls as there is a bug in the Android tool. We often get error saying Failed to Dump Window Hierarchy

8. Android Web apps

8.1 Testing a website on real android phone (Samsung)

Now I am going to show you how we can launch a website on chrome browser in Android. Note that Appium uses selenium webdriver under the hood to automate the web apps.

To update the webdriver.exe, just download it and put it in below directory.
"Appium\node_modules\appium\build\chromedriver\win dows"

Here is the sample program for automating the Android web app. If you are familiar with Selenium Webdriver, below code should be a piece of cake for you to understand.

```
package browsertests;
import org.junit.Test;
import org.openqa.selenium.By;
import org.openqa.selenium.WebDriver;
import org.openqa.selenium.WebElement;
import
org.openqa.selenium.remote.DesiredCapabilities;
import
org.openqa.selenium.remote.RemoteWebDriver;
import org.openqa.selenium.support.ui.Select;
import java.net.URL;
import java.util.concurrent.TimeUnit;
public class LaunchWebsiteOnAndroidPhone
```

```
{
    private WebDriver driver;
    @Test
    public void loadingSinglePageTest() throws
Exception
{
        DesiredCapabilities capabilities = new
DesiredCapabilities();

capabilities.setCapability("platformName",
"Android");

capabilities.setCapability("deviceName",
"sagarcell");
        capabilities.setCapability("app",
"chrome");

capabilities.setCapability("browserName",
"MobileBrowserType.BROWSER");

capabilities.setCapability("platformVersion",
"4.4.4");

//capabilities.setCapability("browserName",
"Chrome");
    driver = new RemoteWebDriver(new
URL("http://127.0.0.1:4723/wd/hub"),
capabilities) {          };

driver.manage().timeouts().implicitlyWait(20,
TimeUnit.SECONDS);
        driver.get("http://www.softpost.org");
        driver.quit();
        //quit the browser
    }
}
```

8.2 Performing Touch actions using TouchActions

We can perform the touch actions in mobile app using below class in Selenium API.

```
org.openqa.selenium.interactions.touch.TouchAct
ions
```

Here is the sample code that illustrates the TouchActions. Note that we can not pass the instance of RemoteWebDriver to the TouchActions class as it does not implement HasTouchScreen interface. So we have created below class that extends the RemoteWebDriver and implements the HasTouchScreen interface.

```
package nativeapptests;
import org.openqa.selenium.Capabilities;
import
org.openqa.selenium.interactions.HasTouchScreen
;
import
org.openqa.selenium.interactions.TouchScreen;
import
org.openqa.selenium.remote.RemoteTouchScreen;
import
org.openqa.selenium.remote.RemoteWebDriver;
import java.net.URL;
/**
 * Created by Sagar on 06-07-2016.
 */
public class MyTouchableWebDriver extends
RemoteWebDriver implements HasTouchScreen
{
    TouchScreen touch;
```

```
   public MyTouchableWebDriver(URL
remoteAddress, Capabilities
desiredCapabilities)
  {
     super(remoteAddress,
desiredCapabilities);
       touch = new
RemoteTouchScreen(getExecuteMethod());
  }
  public TouchScreen getTouch()
  {
    return touch;
  }
}
```

Here is the main test class. Note that we have used singleTap method to build TouchAction object. Alternatively we can also use click method of Selenium.

```
package browsertests;
import nativeapptests.MyTouchableWebDriver;
import org.junit.Test;
import org.openqa.selenium.By;
import org.openqa.selenium.WebDriver;
import
org.openqa.selenium.interactions.touch.TouchAct
ions;
import
org.openqa.selenium.remote.DesiredCapabilities;
import java.net.URL;
import java.util.concurrent.TimeUnit;
public class MyTouchableWebDriverWebTest
{
    private WebDriver driver;
    @Test
```

```
    public void loadingSinglePageTest() throws
Exception
    {
        DesiredCapabilities capabilities = new
DesiredCapabilities();
capabilities.setCapability("platformName",
"Android");

capabilities.setCapability("deviceName",
"sagarcell");
        capabilities.setCapability("app",
"chrome");
        driver = new MyTouchableWebDriver(new
URL("http://127.0.0.1:4723/wd/hub"),
capabilities) {          };

driver.manage().timeouts().implicitlyWait(20,
TimeUnit.SECONDS);
    driver.get("http://www.softpost.org");
        new
TouchActions(driver).singleTap(driver.findEleme
nt(By.linkText("Java"))).build().perform();
        Thread.sleep(5000);
        System.out.println(driver.getTitle());
        driver.close();
        driver.quit();
        //quit the browser
    }
}
```

9. Testing older Android apps using Selendroid in Appium

Note that Appium supports the automation of Android apps in 2 ways.

1. Using Selendroid for Apps with Android API less than 19
2. Using Appium library for latest Android API 19 or more than that

As shown in below image, Appium uses Selendroid to automate the apps running on Honeycomb, Ice Cream Sandwich and Jelly Bean While It uses normal Appium library to automate apps running on KitKat and other latest versions.

Honeycomb[a]	3.0 - 3.2.6	February 22. 2011	11 - 13
Ice Cream Sandwich	4.0 - 4.0.4	October 18, 2011	14 - 15
Jelly Bean	4.1 - 4.3.1	July 9, 2012	16 - 18
KitKat	4.4 - 4.4.4	October 31, 2013	19 - 20
Lollipop	5.0 - 5.1.1	November 12, 2014	21 - 22
Marshmallow	6.0 - 6.0.1	October 5, 2015	23
Nougat	*7.0*	*August or September 2016*	24

Android versions

If you want to test the Android App with API < 19, you can pass below capability.

```
DesiredCapabilities capabilities = new
DesiredCapabilities();
capabilities.setCapability("automationName",
"Selendroid");
```

10. Adding dependency for AndroidDriver

Below dependency is required for AndroidDriver .

```
<dependency>
<groupId>io.appium</groupId>
<artifactId>java-client</artifactId>
<version>3.4.0</version>
</dependency>
```

Once above dependency is added, we can use below classes.

1. AndroidDriver
2. AppiumDriver
3. TouchAction and MultiTouchAction
4. MobileElement

11. Testing a native android application (Installed from .apk)

Now let us take a look at how we can test a native Android application. We are going to automate the calculator that comes with the Android OS.

```java
package nativeapptests;

import org.junit.Assert;
import org.junit.Test;
import org.openqa.selenium.By;
import org.openqa.selenium.WebDriver;
import org.openqa.selenium.WebElement;
import
org.openqa.selenium.remote.DesiredCapabilities;
import
org.openqa.selenium.remote.RemoteWebDriver;

import java.net.URL;
import java.util.concurrent.TimeUnit;

public class LaunchCalculatorOnAndroidPhone
{
    private WebDriver driver;

    @Test
    public void loadingSinglePageTest() throws
Exception
    {
        DesiredCapabilities capabilities = new
DesiredCapabilities();

capabilities.setCapability("platformName",
"Android");
```

```java
capabilities.setCapability("platformVersion",
"4.4.4");

capabilities.setCapability("deviceName",
"sagarcell");

capabilities.setCapability("browser_Name",
"Android");
        // capabilities.setCapability("app",
"chrome");

capabilities.setCapability("appPackage",
"com.sec.android.app.popupcalculator");

capabilities.setCapability("appActivity","com.s
ec.android.app.popupcalculator.Calculator");

//capabilities.setCapability("browserName",
"Chrome");

        driver = new RemoteWebDriver(new
URL("http://127.0.0.1:4723/wd/hub"),
capabilities) {
        };

driver.manage().timeouts().implicitlyWait(20,
TimeUnit.SECONDS);

driver.findElement(By.name("2")).click();


driver.findElement(By.name("+")).click();


driver.findElement(By.name("6")).click();


driver.findElement(By.name("=")).click();
```

```
        WebElement txt=
driver.findElement(By.className("android.widget
.EditText"));

        String p = txt.getText();
        String replacement =
p.replaceAll("\t|\n|\r", "");

Assert.assertTrue("",replacement.equalsIgnoreCa
se("2+6=8"));
        driver.quit();
        //quit the browser
    }
}
```

12. Automating basic tasks

12.1 Simulating back, home button in Android

We can use below lines of code to simulate the back and home button of Android phone in Appium.

To simulate the Home button, we can use below line of code.

```
driver.pressKeyCode(AndroidKeyCode.HOME);
```

To simulate the back button, we can use below lines of code.

```
//driver.navigate().back();
driver.pressKeyCode(AndroidKeyCode.BACK);
```

Here is the complete example on Whatsapp.

```
package nativeapptests;

import io.appium.java_client.TouchAction;
import
io.appium.java_client.android.AndroidDriver;
import
io.appium.java_client.android.AndroidKeyCode;
import org.junit.Test;
import org.openqa.selenium.By;
import org.openqa.selenium.WebElement;
import
org.openqa.selenium.remote.DesiredCapabilities;
import
org.openqa.selenium.support.ui.ExpectedConditio
ns;
import
org.openqa.selenium.support.ui.WebDriverWait;
```

```java
import java.net.URL;
import java.util.concurrent.TimeUnit;

public class SimulateButtonsAndroidPhone
{
    private AndroidDriver driver;

    @Test
    public void test() throws Exception
    {

        DesiredCapabilities capabilities = new
DesiredCapabilities();

capabilities.setCapability("platformName",
"Android");

capabilities.setCapability("platformVersion",
"4.4.4");

capabilities.setCapability("deviceName",
"sagarcell");

capabilities.setCapability("browser_Name",
"Android");

capabilities.setCapability("appPackage",
"com.whatsapp");

capabilities.setCapability("appActivity","com.w
hatsapp.Main");

        try
        {
            driver = new AndroidDriver(new
URL("http://127.0.0.1:4723/wd/hub"),
capabilities) {                };
```

```
driver.manage().timeouts().implicitlyWait(20,
TimeUnit.SECONDS);
            new WebDriverWait(driver,20).

until(ExpectedConditions.elementToBeClickable(B
y.className("android.widget.TextView")));
            WebElement contactsTextViewElement =

driver.findElement(By.className("android.widget
.TextView"));
            driver.performTouchAction(new
TouchAction(driver).tap(contactsTextViewElement
));
            //driver.navigate().back();

driver.pressKeyCode(AndroidKeyCode.BACK);

driver.pressKeyCode(AndroidKeyCode.HOME);
            Thread.sleep(5000);

        }
        catch(Exception ex)
         {
            System.out.println(ex.toString());
         }
        finally
        {
            //quit the browser
            driver.quit();
        }
    }
}
```

12.2 Synchronization in Android

For web apps and Webview Contexts, we can use normal Selenium methods to add synchronization points in the script.

For Native controls in the App, we can use implicitlyWait and wait conditions (explicit wait) but can not use pageLoadTimeout method.

12.3 Taking a screenshot in Appium

Now let us learn how to take the screenshot in Appium.

We can take the screenshot of an Android app as illustrated in below code. Note that we are using selenium API for taking a screenshot.

```java
package nativeapptests;

import org.apache.commons.io.FileUtils;
import org.junit.Assert;
import org.junit.Test;
import org.openqa.selenium.*;
import
org.openqa.selenium.remote.DesiredCapabilities;
import
org.openqa.selenium.remote.RemoteWebDriver;

import java.io.File;
import java.net.URL;
import java.util.concurrent.TimeUnit;

public class LaunchCalculatorOnAndroidPhone
```

```
{
    private WebDriver driver;

    @Test
    public void loadingSinglePageTest() throws
Exception
    {
        DesiredCapabilities capabilities = new
DesiredCapabilities();

capabilities.setCapability("platformName",
"Android");

capabilities.setCapability("platformVersion",
"4.4.4");

capabilities.setCapability("deviceName",
"sagarcell");

capabilities.setCapability("browser_Name",
"Android");
        // capabilities.setCapability("app",
"chrome");

capabilities.setCapability("appPackage",
"com.sec.android.app.popupcalculator");

capabilities.setCapability("appActivity","com.s
ec.android.app.popupcalculator.Calculator");

//capabilities.setCapability("browserName",
"Chrome");

        driver = new RemoteWebDriver(new
URL("http://127.0.0.1:4723/wd/hub"),
capabilities) {          };

driver.manage().timeouts().implicitlyWait(20,
TimeUnit.SECONDS);
```

```
driver.findElement(By.name("2")).click();

driver.findElement(By.name("+")).click();

driver.findElement(By.name("6")).click();

driver.findElement(By.name("=")).click();
        WebElement txt=
driver.findElement(By.className("android.widget
.EditText"));

        File f = ((TakesScreenshot)
driver).getScreenshotAs(OutputType.FILE);

        try
        {
            FileUtils.copyFile(f,
                    new
File("C:\\Users\\Sagar\\IdeaProjects\\AndroidAu
tomation\\abc.png"));
        }
        catch(Exception ex)
        {
            System.out.println("Exception " +
ex.toString());
        }

        String p = txt.getText();
        String replacement =
p.replaceAll("\t|\n|\r", "");

Assert.assertTrue("",replacement.equalsIgnoreCa
se("2+6=8"));
        driver.quit();
        //quit the browser
    }
}
```

Here is the screenshot of calculator.

Calculator screenshot using Appium - Selenium

Please note that if you are using selenium grid, you will have to use below code to take the screenshot.

```java
WebDriver augmentedDriver = new
Augmenter().augment(driver);

  File f = ((TakesScreenshot) augmentedDriver
).getScreenshotAs(OutputType.FILE);

      try
      {
            FileUtils.copyFile(f,
                    new
File("C:\\Users\\Sagar\\IdeaProjects\\AndroidAu
tomation\\abc.png"));
      }
      catch(Exception ex)
      {
            System.out.println("Exception " +
ex.toString());
      }
```

13. Testing the hybrid Android application

Testing the Hybrid apps is very simple. All you have to do is switch the context to Webview and perform normal selenium operations. Note that Webview debugging should be enabled in the app by developer otherwise you will not be able to switch the context to Webview.

```java
package hybridtests;

import
io.appium.java_client.android.AndroidDriver;
import org.junit.Test;
import
org.openqa.selenium.remote.DesiredCapabilities;

import java.net.URL;
import java.util.concurrent.TimeUnit;

public class LaunchLocaleur
{
    private AndroidDriver driver;
@Test
public void test() throws Exception
{
    DesiredCapabilities capabilities = new
DesiredCapabilities();
    capabilities.setCapability("platformName",
"Android");

capabilities.setCapability("platformVersion",
"4.4.4");
    capabilities.setCapability("deviceName",
"sagarcell");
    capabilities.setCapability("browser_Name",
"Android");
```

```java
    capabilities.setCapability("appPackage",
"package1");

capabilities.setCapability("appActivity","Activ
ityName");

    driver = new AndroidDriver(new
URL("http://127.0.0.1:4723/wd/hub"),
capabilities) {
    };

driver.manage().timeouts().implicitlyWait(20,
TimeUnit.SECONDS);

    //get contexts
    //If your app has got any WebViews, count
should be more than 1.
    System.out.println("Context count " +
driver.getContextHandles().size());

    for (Object contextName :
driver.getContextHandles())
    {
        System.out.println("Context Name -> " +
contextName);
        if
(contextName.toString().toUpperCase().contains(
"WEBVIEW"))
        {

driver.context(contextName.toString());
            System.out.println("Switched to
WebView Context");
        }
    }

    driver.get("http://www.softpost.org");
    driver.close();

    //Switch back to Native app
```

```
    driver.context("NATIVE_APP");
    driver.quit();
}
}
```

14. Important classes in Appium library

14.1 AppiumDriver

AppiumDriver class provides below methods.

AndroidDriver and IOSDriver classes inherit this class.

1. closeApp - used to close the application under test
2. context - used to switch the context from WebView to Native and vice versa
3. findElementsByAccessibilityId - used to identify the elements using accessibility id
4. getContext - used to get the current context of the App
5. getContextHandles - used to get the total number of context handles
6. getOrientation - used to get the device orientation - Portrait or Landscape
7. getRemoteAddress - used to get the remote address of device
8. hideKeyboard - used to hide the keyboard
9. installApp - used to install the app on device
10. performMultiTouchAction - used to perform multiple touch actions at the same time

14.2 AndroidDriver

AndroidDriver class provides below methods in Appium.

1. swipe - swipes the app from point A to point B
2. findElementsByAndroidUIAutomator
3. context - used to switch contexts
4. currentActivity - gets the current activity of app
5. pressKeyCode - used to press the Key code
6. longPressKeyCode - used to long press key code
7. closeApp - closes down the app
8. launchApp - launches app
9. isLocked - checks if device is locked
10. lockDevice - locks the device
11. zoom - zooms the particular point on the screen
12. tap - taps on specific element or location on screen
13. openNotifications - opens notification screen
14. startActivity - starts the activity in app
15. rotate - roatates the screen orientation - landscape or protrait
16. resetApp - resets the App
17. pinch - pinches the screen location
18. installApp - installs the app on device

14.3 MobileElement

MobileElement class can be used to perform below operations.

1. pinch - used to pinch the element in App
2. zoom - used to zoom on the element in the App
3. swipe - used to swipe the screen on the device
4. tap - used to tap on the mobile element
5. getCenter - used to get the center co-ordinates of the element.

15. Complex actions in Appium

15.1 Finding the center position of an element

Below example shows how to find the center position of
an element in Android app using Appium. It also shows
how to find the X and Y co-ordinates of the top left corner
of the element.

```java
package nativeapptests;

import io.appium.java_client.MobileElement;
import io.appium.java_client.TouchAction;
import io.appium.java_client.android.AndroidDriver;
import org.junit.Test;
import org.openqa.selenium.By;
import org.openqa.selenium.WebElement;
import org.openqa.selenium.remote.DesiredCapabilities;
import org.openqa.selenium.support.ui.ExpectedConditions;
import org.openqa.selenium.support.ui.WebDriverWait;

import java.net.URL;
import java.util.concurrent.TimeUnit;

public class FindingPositionOnAndroidPhone
{
    private AndroidDriver driver;

    @Test
    public void test() throws Exception
    {
```

```
      DesiredCapabilities capabilities = new
DesiredCapabilities();

capabilities.setCapability("platformName",
"Android");

capabilities.setCapability("platformVersion",
"4.4.4");

capabilities.setCapability("deviceName",
"sagarcell");

capabilities.setCapability("browser_Name",
"Android");

capabilities.setCapability("appPackage",
"com.whatsapp");

capabilities.setCapability("appActivity","com.w
hatsapp.Main");

        try
        {
            driver = new AndroidDriver(new
URL("http://127.0.0.1:4723/wd/hub"),
capabilities) {                };


driver.manage().timeouts().implicitlyWait(20,
TimeUnit.SECONDS);
            new WebDriverWait(driver,20).

until(ExpectedConditions.elementToBeClickable(B
y.className("android.widget.TextView")));
            WebElement contactsTextViewElement =

driver.findElement(By.className("android.widget
.TextView"));
```

```
            System.out.println("X co-ordinate
of TextView "
                +
contactsTextViewElement.getLocation().getX());
            System.out.println("Y co-ordinate
of TextView "
                +
contactsTextViewElement.getLocation().getY());

            System.out.println("X co-ordinate
of center of TextView "
                +
((MobileElement)contactsTextViewElement).getCen
ter().getX());
            System.out.println("Y co-ordinate
of center of TextView "
                +
((MobileElement)contactsTextViewElement).getCen
ter().getY());

        }
      catch(Exception ex)
      {
            System.out.println(ex.toString());
      }
      finally
      {
          //quit the browser
          driver.quit();
      }
    }
}
```

Here is the output of above code.

X co-ordinate of TextView 123

Y co-ordinate of TextView 216

X co-ordinate of center of TextView 154

Y co-ordinate of center of TextView 234

15.2 Swiping horizontally

Below example illustrates how to swipe the app screen in Appium. Below code can be used to swipe horizontally on Whatsapp Android app is given below.

```java
package nativeapptests;

import
io.appium.java_client.android.AndroidDriver;
import org.junit.Test;
import org.openqa.selenium.By;
import org.openqa.selenium.Dimension;
import org.openqa.selenium.WebElement;
import
org.openqa.selenium.remote.DesiredCapabilities;

import java.net.URL;
import java.util.concurrent.TimeUnit;

public class SwipingTestInWhatsapp
{
    private AndroidDriver driver;

    @Test
    public void loadingSinglePageTest() throws
Exception
    {
```

```
        DesiredCapabilities capabilities = new
DesiredCapabilities();

capabilities.setCapability("platformName",
"Android");

capabilities.setCapability("platformVersion",
"4.4.4");

capabilities.setCapability("deviceName",
"sagarcell");

capabilities.setCapability("browser_Name",
"Android");
            // capabilities.setCapability("app",
"chrome");

capabilities.setCapability("appPackage",
"com.whatsapp");

capabilities.setCapability("appActivity","com.w
hatsapp.Main");

//capabilities.setCapability("browserName",
"Chrome");


        try
        {
            driver = new AndroidDriver(new
URL("http://127.0.0.1:4723/wd/hub"),
capabilities) {              };


driver.manage().timeouts().implicitlyWait(20,
TimeUnit.SECONDS);
            Thread.sleep(5000);


            Dimension size =
driver.manage().window().getSize();
```

```
            System.out.println("App window
dimensions -> " + size);

            //swiping from left to right
            driver.swipe(1,   size.height/2,
size.width-1,  size.height/2, 2000);
            Thread.sleep(2000);

            //swiping from right to left
            driver.swipe(size.width-1,
size.height/2, 1,  size.height/2, 2000);
            Thread.sleep(2000);

        }
    catch(Exception ex)
    {
            System.out.println(ex.toString());


    }
    finally
    {
            //quit the browser
            driver.quit();
    }

    }
}
```

15.3 Swiping vertically

Below example illustrates how to swipe vertically in Android app.

```java
package nativeapptests;

import
io.appium.java_client.android.AndroidDriver;
import org.junit.Test;
import org.openqa.selenium.Dimension;
import
org.openqa.selenium.remote.DesiredCapabilities;

import java.net.URL;
import java.util.concurrent.TimeUnit;

public class SwipingTestVerticallyInWhatsapp
{
    private AndroidDriver driver;

    @Test
    public void loadingSinglePageTest() throws
Exception
    {

        DesiredCapabilities capabilities = new
DesiredCapabilities();

capabilities.setCapability("platformName",
"Android");

capabilities.setCapability("platformVersion",
"4.4.4");

capabilities.setCapability("deviceName",
"sagarcell");

capabilities.setCapability("browser_Name",
"Android");
```

```java
      // capabilities.setCapability("app",
"chrome");

capabilities.setCapability("appPackage",
"com.whatsapp");

capabilities.setCapability("appActivity","com.w
hatsapp.Main");

//capabilities.setCapability("browserName",
"Chrome");

       try
       {
           driver = new AndroidDriver(new
URL("http://127.0.0.1:4723/wd/hub"),
capabilities) {             };


driver.manage().timeouts().implicitlyWait(20,
TimeUnit.SECONDS);
           Thread.sleep(5000);


           Dimension size =
driver.manage().window().getSize();
           System.out.println("App window
dimensions -> " + size);
           driver.swipe(size.width/2,
size.height-1, size.width/2,200   , 2000);

           //swiping from top to bottom
           Thread.sleep(2000);

           //swiping from bottom to top
            driver.swipe(size.width/2,  200,
size.width/2,  size.height-1, 2000);

           Thread.sleep(2000);
```

```
        }
    catch(Exception ex)
    {
        System.out.println(ex.toString());


    }
    finally
    {
        //quit the browser
        driver.quit();
    }

    }
}
```

15.4 Tapping on an element

Below example illustrates how to tap on an element in an Android app in Appium. Note that we have used io.appium.java_client.TouchAction class to tap on an element.

```
package nativeapptests;

import io.appium.java_client.TouchAction;
import
io.appium.java_client.android.AndroidDriver;
import org.junit.Test;
import org.openqa.selenium.By;
import org.openqa.selenium.Dimension;
import org.openqa.selenium.WebElement;
import
org.openqa.selenium.remote.DesiredCapabilities;
```

```
import
org.openqa.selenium.support.ui.ExpectedConditio
ns;
import
org.openqa.selenium.support.ui.WebDriverWait;

import java.net.URL;
import java.util.concurrent.TimeUnit;

public class
TappingElementInWhatsappOnAndroidPhone
{
    private AndroidDriver driver;

    @Test
    public void tapTest() throws Exception
    {

        DesiredCapabilities capabilities = new
DesiredCapabilities();

capabilities.setCapability("platformName",
"Android");

capabilities.setCapability("platformVersion",
"4.4.4");

capabilities.setCapability("deviceName",
"sagarcell");

capabilities.setCapability("browser_Name",
"Android");

capabilities.setCapability("appPackage",
"com.whatsapp");

capabilities.setCapability("appActivity","com.w
hatsapp.Main");
        try
        {
```

```
            driver = new AndroidDriver(new
URL("http://127.0.0.1:4723/wd/hub"),
capabilities) {              };


driver.manage().timeouts().implicitlyWait(20,
TimeUnit.SECONDS);
        new WebDriverWait(driver,20).

until(ExpectedConditions.elementToBeClickable(B
y.className("android.widget.TextView")));
        WebElement contactsTextViewElement =

driver.findElement(By.className("android.widget
.TextView"));

        //You can use TouchAction Class
        //new
TouchAction(driver).tap(contactsTextViewElement
).perform();

        //or you can also use below syntax
        driver.performTouchAction(new
TouchAction(driver).tap(contactsTextViewElement
));

    }
  catch(Exception ex)
  {
      System.out.println(ex.toString());
  }
  finally
  {
      //quit the browser
      driver.quit();
  }
 }
}
```

15.5 Long pressing an element

Below example illustrates how to long press an element and simply press an element in Android App in Appium. As you can see, we have used TouchAction class to press an element.

```
package nativeapptests;

import io.appium.java_client.TouchAction;
import
io.appium.java_client.android.AndroidDriver;
import org.junit.Test;
import org.openqa.selenium.By;
import org.openqa.selenium.WebElement;
import
org.openqa.selenium.remote.DesiredCapabilities;
import
org.openqa.selenium.support.ui.ExpectedConditio
ns;
import
org.openqa.selenium.support.ui.WebDriverWait;

import java.net.URL;
import java.util.concurrent.TimeUnit;

public class
PressingElementInWhatsappOnAndroidPhone
{
    private AndroidDriver driver;

    @Test
    public void tapTest() throws Exception
    {

        DesiredCapabilities capabilities = new
DesiredCapabilities();
```

```java
capabilities.setCapability("platformName",
"Android");

capabilities.setCapability("platformVersion",
"4.4.4");

capabilities.setCapability("deviceName",
"sagarcell");

capabilities.setCapability("browser_Name",
"Android");

capabilities.setCapability("appPackage",
"com.whatsapp");

capabilities.setCapability("appActivity","com.w
hatsapp.Main");

        try
        {
            driver = new AndroidDriver(new
URL("http://127.0.0.1:4723/wd/hub"),
capabilities) {            };


driver.manage().timeouts().implicitlyWait(20,
TimeUnit.SECONDS);
            new WebDriverWait(driver,20).

until(ExpectedConditions.elementToBeClickable(B
y.className("android.widget.TextView")));
            WebElement contactsTextViewElement =

driver.findElement(By.className("android.widget
.TextView")));

            //long press the first chat contact
in whatsapp
```

```
                new
TouchAction(driver).longPress(contactsTextViewE
lement,2000);

                //press (tap) the first contact in
whatsapp
                new
TouchAction(driver).press(contactsTextViewEleme
nt);

        }
        catch(Exception ex)
        {
                System.out.println(ex.toString());
        }
        finally
        {
                //quit the browser
                driver.quit();
        }
    }
}
```

15.6 Performing multiple actions simultaneously

We can perform multiple actions using MultiTouchAction class in Appium. Below code shows how to add actions to MultiTouchAction class and then perform all actions at the same time.

In below example, we are moving the element e1 to e2 and at the same time moving the element e3 to e4 at the same time. Also note how we have used waitAction which is used to wait for specific period of time.

```
TouchAction action1 = new TouchAction(driver);
action1.longPress(e1).moveTo(e2).waitAction(100
).release();

TouchAction action2 = new TouchAction(driver);
action2.longPress(e3).moveTo(e4).waitAction(100
).release();

new
MultiTouchAction(driver).add(action1).add(actio
n2).perform();
```

15.7 Perform Pinch and Zoom action

Below example shows how to perform pinch action in Appium.

We can use pinch and zoom methods of AndroidDriver to pinch or zoom in Android app using Appium. Below code will launch camera on Android phone and then zoom and pinch the screen.

```
package nativeapptests;

import
io.appium.java_client.android.AndroidDriver;
import org.junit.Test;
import org.openqa.selenium.By;
import org.openqa.selenium.Dimension;
import org.openqa.selenium.WebElement;
import
org.openqa.selenium.remote.DesiredCapabilities;

import java.net.URL;
```

```
import java.util.concurrent.TimeUnit;

public class CameraTest
{
    private AndroidDriver driver;

    @Test
    public void test1() throws Exception
    {

        DesiredCapabilities capabilities = new
DesiredCapabilities();

capabilities.setCapability("platformName",
"Android");

capabilities.setCapability("platformVersion",
"4.4.4");

capabilities.setCapability("deviceName",
"sagarcell");

capabilities.setCapability("browser_Name",
"Android");

capabilities.setCapability("appPackage",
"com.sec.android.app.camera");

capabilities.setCapability("appActivity","com.s
ec.android.app.camera.Camera");

        try
        {
            driver = new AndroidDriver(new
URL("http://127.0.0.1:4723/wd/hub"),
capabilities) {            };

driver.manage().timeouts().implicitlyWait(20,
TimeUnit.SECONDS);
            Thread.sleep(5000);
```

```
          WebElement e=
driver.findElement(By.className("android.widget
.LinearLayout"));
          driver.zoom(e);
          Thread.sleep(5000);
          driver.pinch(e);
          Thread.sleep(5000);
      }
      catch(Exception ex)
      {
          System.out.println(ex.toString());
      }
      finally
      {
          //quit the browser
          driver.quit();
      }

   }
}
```

16. Android Emulator Automation

16.1 How to install the Intel x86 Emulator Accelerator (HAXM)

When we launch the Android virtual device, we often get the error saying -

emulator: ERROR: x86 emulation currently requires hardware acceleration!

Please ensure Intel HAXM is properly installed and usable.

CPU acceleration status: HAX kernel module is not installed!

To fix above error, You need to open Android SDK Manager and Download Intel x86 Emulator Accelerator (HAXM installer)
Then Go to below directory within Android installation directory

extras/intel/Hardware_Accelerated_Execution_Manager and run below file

"intelhaxm-android.exe"

This is required to fast track the booting process of the Android Emulator.

 Note that only computers with Intel processors have virtualization technology. You can enable it from the boot menu of your system.

16.2 Testing Android apps on Emulators (Virtual devices)

Appium can be used to test the android applications running on Emulators. You need to follow below steps to create the emulator in Windows.

1. Download and install Android SDK
2. Create AVD - Android Virtual Device using AVD manager and Start it
3. Start the Appium server
4. From the code, you can pass the name of the AVD device in deviceName capability.

Here is the sample code to launch the calculator app on Emulator.

```
package nativeapptests;

import
io.appium.java_client.android.AndroidDriver;
import org.apache.commons.io.FileUtils;
import org.junit.Assert;
import org.junit.Test;
import org.openqa.selenium.By;
import org.openqa.selenium.OutputType;
import org.openqa.selenium.TakesScreenshot;
import org.openqa.selenium.WebElement;
import
org.openqa.selenium.remote.DesiredCapabilities;

import java.io.File;
import java.net.URL;
import java.util.concurrent.TimeUnit;

public class LaunchCalculatorOnEmulator
{
    private AndroidDriver driver;

    @Test
    public void loadingSinglePageTest() throws
Exception
    {
        DesiredCapabilities capabilities = new
DesiredCapabilities();

capabilities.setCapability("platformName",
"Android");

capabilities.setCapability("platformVersion",
"4.4.4");
```

```
capabilities.setCapability("deviceName",
"AVD1");

capabilities.setCapability("browser_Name",
"Android");

capabilities.setCapability("appPackage",
"com.android.calculator2");

capabilities.setCapability("appActivity","com.a
ndroid.calculator2.Calculator");

//capabilities.setCapability("browserName",
"Chrome");

        driver = new AndroidDriver(new
URL("http://127.0.0.1:4723/wd/hub"),
capabilities) {          };

driver.manage().timeouts().implicitlyWait(20,
TimeUnit.SECONDS);

driver.findElement(By.name("2")).click();


driver.findElement(By.name("+")).click();


driver.findElement(By.name("6")).click();


driver.findElement(By.name("=")).click();
        WebElement txt=
driver.findElement(By.className("android.widget
.EditText"));

        String p = txt.getText();
        String replacement =
p.replaceAll("\t|\n|\r", "");
```

```
Assert.assertTrue("",replacement.equalsIgnoreCa
se("2+6=8"));

        driver.quit();
        //quit the browser
    }
}
```

17. Registering appium (Android node) with Selenium grid

We can use below command to register appium with Selenium Grid.

node appium --nodeconfig android.json -p 4723 -U sagarcell -a 127.0.0.1 --no-reset

Here are the contents of android.json file.

```
{
"capabilities":
[
{
"deviceName": "sagarcell",
"browserName": "Android",
"version":"4.4.4",
"maxInstances": 1,
"platform":"ANDROID"
}
],
"configuration":
```

```json
{

"cleanUpCycle":300000,

"timeout":400000,

"proxy":
"org.openqa.grid.selenium.proxy.DefaultRemotePr
oxy",

"url":"http://localhost:4730/wd/hub",

"maxSession": 1,

"port": "4730",

"host": "127.0.0.1",

"register": true,

"registerCycle": 2000,

"hubPort": "4444",

"hubHost": "127.0.0.1"

}

}
```

iOS automation Testing

18. Setting up Appium environment in Mac OS X

You can follow below steps to set up the Appium environment in Mac OS X.

You can install Appium.app from http://appium.io/downloads.html and start the server from GUI. It's that simple.

But you can install the appium from command line as well. You will need below software tools

1. Mac OSX 10.7 or higher
2. Xcode > 4.6.3 (Note that Xcode also installs the simulators like iPhone, iPad ect)
3. Command line build tools from within Xcode - https://developer.apple.com/library/ios/technotes /tn2339/_index.html
    Java

Xcode icon

Xcode showing version

Here are the commands to install node and appium.

brew install node

npm install -g appium

appium &

To uninstall appium, use below command.

npm uninstall -g appium

To kill the appium server, use below command

ps aux | grep appium

kill -9 <process id>

19. Installing appium app on Mac OS X

Below images show how to install the appium app in Mac OS X. You need to download the appium.dmg file from the Appium website - http://appium.io/downloads.html.

After downloading the file, extract it and put appium.app in Applications directory. Then start the appium. When you start the appium for the first time, you will be asked to authorize appium to run the iOS Simulator. Click on Yes.

Authorize the appium to use iOS simulators like iPhone and iPads

Below image shows the general settings of the Appium
server. We can specify below things on this screen.

1. Server address and port - This is the address you
   pass to RemoteWebDriver or AndroidDriver
   constructor in the code.
2. Whether to override the session
3. Command timeout duration
4. Logging settings

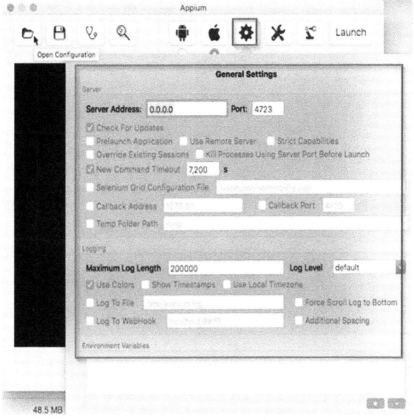

General settings of Appium

Below image shows Android settings. We can specify below things on this screen.

1. Application path, package name, activity name
2. Platform Name and version
3. Device name
4. Automation name
5. Whether to reset the app or not

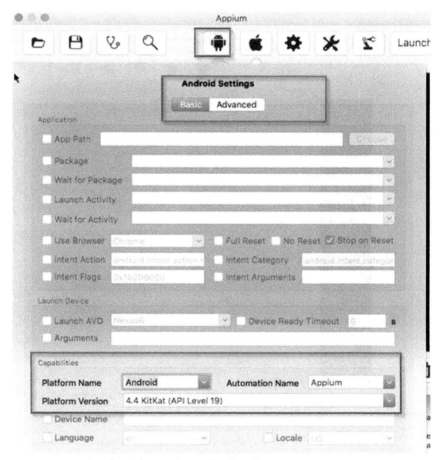

Android settings in Appium app

Below image shows iOS settings you can configure in
Appium.

1. Application path
2. Bundle Id of the app
3. Platform version
4. Device name
5. Whether to reset the app or not

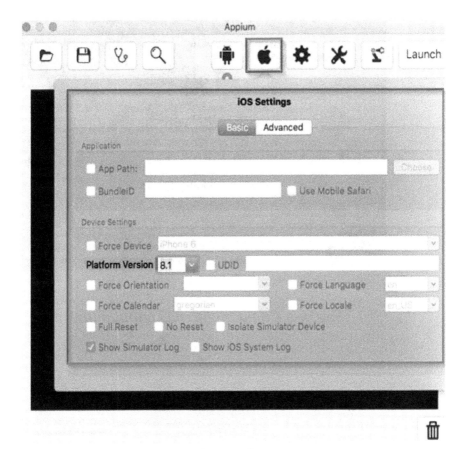

iOS settings in Appium app

Below image shows sample log when Appium server is started with iOS capabilities.

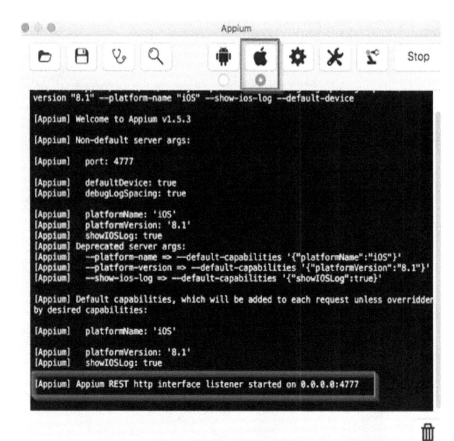

Starting Appium with iOS capabilities

Below image shows sample log when Appium server is started with Android capabilities.

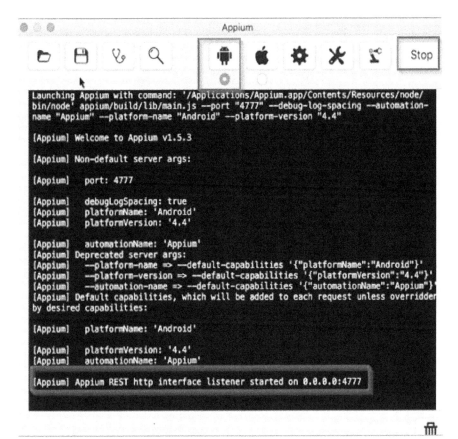

Starting Appium with Android capabilities

20. Appium doctor

Appium doctor is used to check if all tools are set up properly in Mac OS X.

Appium doctor checks below things.

1. Xcode and command line tools are installed or not?
2. DevToolsSecurity is enabled or not
3. ANDROID_HOME and JAVA_HOME variables are set or not?
4. Android tools like adb, android and emulator exists or not

If all tools are installed correctly, you will see message saying - Everything looks ok

21. Simulators in XCode

You can open simulator window by selecting below menu options in Xcode.

Xcode -> Open Developer Tool -> Simulator

To view all available simulator devices, you can select below menu options in Simulator window.

Hardware -> Device

When you launch the simulator, you can see platform version at the top as shown in below image.

iPhone Simulator showing the version

22. Capabilities for iOS automation

Here are some of the capabilities you can pass.

1. platformName
2. platformVersion
3. deviceName
4. app
5. bundleId
6. safariAllowPopups
7. autoAcceptAlerts

Here is the sample code to launch the app on iPhone 6 on iOS 9.

```
DesiredCapabilities cap = new
DesiredCapabilities();
cap.setCapability("platformName", "iOS");
cap.setCapability("platformVersion", "9.0");
cap.setCapability("deviceName", "iPhone 6");
cap.setCapability("app", /usr/my.app");
```

To run tests on safari browser, you will have to pass below capability.

capabilities.setCapability(MobileCapabilityType.BROWSER
_NAME, "Safari");

In the device name, you can give values like iPhone 4s, iPhone 5, iPhone 5s, iPhone 6, iPhone 6 Plus, iPhone 6s, iPhone 6s Plus, iPad 2, iPad Retina, iPad Air, iPad Air 2, iPad Pro etc. depending upon what all simulators are available in your Xcode.

If you want to automate the app on real iOS device, you need to pass below capability.

capabilities.setCapability(MobileCapabilityType.UDID, "fhg87878hjhj86");

23. Inpsecting the elements from Appium inspector

We can inspect the elements inside iOS app using inspector tool provided in Appium GUI. First of all start the appium server with iOS capabilities. Then you can use inspector.

Below image shows how to start the inspector tool.

Inspector in Appium

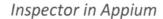

Below image shows how Appium inspector shows the
elements within iOS app.

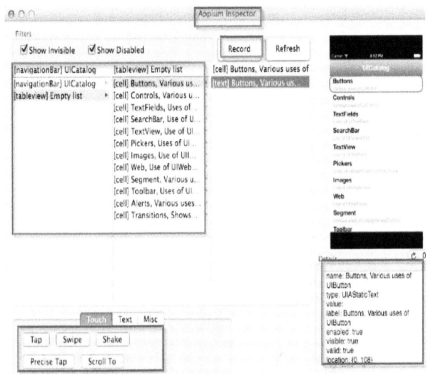

iOS inspector showing app elements

24. Automating Native iOS app

Here is the simple example to test the app on iPhone simulator. To run scripts on real iOS device, you will need one more capability - 'UDID' (Device ID)

```
package iostests;

import io.appium.java_client.ios.IOSDriver;
import org.junit.Test;
import org.openqa.selenium.By;
import
org.openqa.selenium.remote.DesiredCapabilities;

import java.net.URL;

/**
 * Created by Sagar on 10-07-2016.
 */
public class NativeAppTest
{
    IOSDriver driver;
    @Test
    public void test1() throws Exception
    {
        DesiredCapabilities caps = new
DesiredCapabilities();
        caps.setCapability("platformName",
"iOS");
        caps.setCapability("platformVersion",
"9.0");
        caps.setCapability("deviceName",
"iPhone 6s");
        caps.setCapability("app",
"/usr/myapp1.app");
        driver = new IOSDriver(new
URL("http://0.0.0.0:4723/wd/hub"), caps);
```

```
driver.findElement(By.xpath("//UIAStaticText[3]
")).click();
        driver.quit();
    }

}
```

25. Automating iOS Hybrid app

We can automate the hybrid app very easily using Appium. Hybrid app contains native control as well as web controls. You need to switch the context to web control within app and then we can use the normal Selenium webdriver API to perform the operations.

To auto switch the context to web, you can pass below capability.

capabilities.SetCapability("autoWebview", true);

Otherwise you can use below code to find all contexts within app and switch to it.

```
System.out.println("Context count " +
driver.getContextHandles().size());

    for (Object contextName :
driver.getContextHandles())
    {
        System.out.println("Context Name -> " +
contextName);
        if
(contextName.toString().toUpperCase().contains(
"WEBVIEW"))
        {

driver.context(contextName.toString());
            System.out.println("Switched to
WebView Context");
```

```
        }
    }
    driver.get("http://www.softpost.org");
    driver.close();

    //Switch back to Native app
    driver.context("NATIVE_APP");
```

26. Automating Web app

Here is the example that shows how to automate web app on iOS device using Appium. Below code will launch safari in iPad and then open www.softpost.org website. Note that Automating the web app on iOS device is similar to automating the website on desktop browser.

```java
package iostests;

import io.appium.java_client.ios.IOSDriver;
import org.junit.Test;
import org.openqa.selenium.By;
import
org.openqa.selenium.remote.CapabilityType;
import
org.openqa.selenium.remote.DesiredCapabilities;

import java.net.URL;
import java.util.concurrent.TimeUnit;

/**
 * Created by Sagar on 10-07-2016.
 */
public class WebAppTest
{
    IOSDriver driver;
    @Test
    public void test1() throws Exception
    {
        DesiredCapabilities caps = new
DesiredCapabilities();
        caps.setCapability("platformName",
"iOS");
        caps.setCapability("platformVersion",
"9.0");
```

```
        caps.setCapability("deviceName", "iPad
pro");

caps.setCapability(CapabilityType.BROWSER_NAME,
"safari");
        driver = new IOSDriver(new
URL("http://0.0.0.0:4723/wd/hub"), caps);

driver.manage().timeouts().implicitlyWait(20,
TimeUnit.SECONDS);
        driver.get("http://www.softpost.org");
        driver.close();
        driver.quit();
    }

}
```

27. Hooking up appium with Selenium grid

You can register appium node with Selenium hub by using below command.

appium --nodeconfig iOSConfig.json -p 4723 -U 4df70d325d884031 -a 127.0.0.1

Here are the contents of iOSConfig.json file.

```
{

    "capabilities": [

        {

            "browserName": "iPhone-Simulator",

            "version": "9.0",

            "maxInstances": 1,

            "platform": "MAC"

        }

    ],

    "configuration": {

        "cleanUpCycle": 3000,

        "timeout": 400000,
```

```json
        "browserTimeout": 70000,

        "hub":
"http://localhost:4444/grid/register",

        "host": " 127.0.0.1",

        "maxSession": 1,

        "port": 4723,

        "hubPort": 4444,

        "hubHost": "127.0.0.1",

        "url": "http://127.0.0.1:4723/wd/hub",

      "register": true,

      "registerCycle": 6000,

        "role": "node"

    }

}
```

www.ingramcontent.com/pod-product-compliance
Lightning Source LLC
Chambersburg PA
CBHW071222050326
40689CB00011B/2406